Mount Rushmore

From Mountain to Monument

Mount Rushmore

From Mountain to Monument

★ ★ ★ **Luke S. Gabriel**

THE CHILD'S WORLD®, INC.

Library of Congress Cataloging-in-Publication Data
Gabriel, Luke, S.
Mount Rushmore : from mountain to monument / by Luke S. Gabriel.
p.   cm.
Includes index.
Summary: Describes the creation of the huge sculpture carved into
Mt. Rushmore in the 1920s under the direction of Gutzon Borglum.
ISBN 1-56766-763-5
1. Mount Rushmore National Memorial (S.D.)—Juvenile literature.
2. Borglum, Gutzon, 1867-1941—Juvenile literature.
[1. Mount Rushmore National Memorial (S.D.) 2. National monuments.]   I. Title.
F657.R8 G34   2000
978.3'93—dc21   99-054207

Credits

© Bell Studio: 24
© Bruce Leighty/The Image Finders: 29, 30
© Charles D'Emery: 6
© Christan Heeb/Gnass Photo Images: cover
© Della B. Vic: 10
© Ira S. Rubin: 9, 16
© Jon Gnass/Gnass Photo Images: 19
© Lincoln Borglum Collection: 15, 23
© Publisher's Photo Service: 20 (bottom)
© Rise Studio, Rapid City, South Dakota: 13, 20 (top), 26
© William J. Weber/Visuals Unlimited: 2

On the cover...

Front cover: This picture of Mount Rushmore was taken on a clear August morning.
Page 2: Here you can see Mount Rushmore from farther away.

Chapter	Page

"Higher, higher!" This is the command of a worker carving a huge stone face. The year is 1935. The face is being carved on the top of a mountain called Mount Rushmore. Mount Rushmore is a part of the Black Hills of western South Dakota. A giant carving called a **monument** was being created. But why was a monument being carved on the top of a South Dakota mountain? That's what many people wanted to know.

⇐ **Rushmore's sculptor, Gutzon Borglum, hangs from a chair near the mountain.**

It all started in 1923. That was when a man named Doane Robinson had an idea. He thought that a huge monument should be created in the Black Hills to mark the end of the Great Plains and beginning of the Rocky Mountains. This monument would show how much the United States had grown over the last 150 years.

Many people didn't like the idea because of the cost. They also thought the mountains should be left alone. Eventually people agreed and the project began in 1927. But who would be chosen to make the monument?

The best view of the four faces is ⇒ from the front of the mountain.

In 1867, a boy named Gutzon Borglum was born in Bear Lake, Idaho. He wanted to be an artist. His brother was an artist. When he grew up, Gutzon went to Paris to study art. The type of art he liked best was called sculpting. A **sculptor** is an artist who carves statues out of stone or other materials.

When Gutzon moved back to the United States, he started making sculptures. He carved statues for a **cathedral,** or big church, in New York City. He was chosen to carve a big statue of President Lincoln at the Capitol in Washington, D.C. In 1915, Gutzon was chosen to carve a giant sculpture on Stone Mountain in Georgia. He became known as the "Giant Sculpture Maker." Because he was such a good sculptor, Gutzon was chosen to carve the monument in the Black Hills.

⇐ **Gutzon Borglum takes a break from sculpting to get his picture taken.**

At first, some people thought a monument should be carved in a part of the Black Hills called *The Needles.* The Needles were tall mountains that stood together in a row. People thought that famous explorers or Native American Indian chiefs could be carved in the tops of the Needles.

Gutzon wandered around the Black Hills and saw a better place to build the monument. This was Mount Rushmore. The **peak** or top of this mountain was more than 6,000 feet high. It was made of hard rock called **granite.** It faced towards the sun most of the day, so Gutzon thought it would be perfect.

This is what the mountain looked ⇒ like before the faces were carved.

But what type of monument should be carved? Gutzon looked at the mountain and got the idea to carve the faces of four presidents. He thought faces would fit nicely into the shape of the mountain. Because this was going to be a monument for the whole country, he thought he should carve the faces of leaders of our country. He talked with many people but couldn't easily decide which presidents to pick. Choosing which presidents to carve was a very important decision!

Borglum created this smaller sculpture to get an ⇒ idea of how he wanted the monument to look.

So how did Gutzon pick the four presidents? The mountain could fit four faces, and Gutzon wanted to pick the four presidents who most helped the United States grow. He wanted presidents who were important in shaping the first 150 years of the nation's history.

He picked George Washington and gave him the highest and most important spot on the mountain. That was because Washington was our first president and led the United States in the Revolutionary War. Gutzon carved Washington's head on the far left side of the mountain.

⇐ **Borglum even carved details such as eyebrows and hair on Washington's head.**

Gutzon picked Thomas Jefferson and carved his head next. Jefferson was chosen because he wrote the Declaration of Independence. He was the third president of the United States and helped our country expand west. Jefferson's head is next to Washington's.

On the right side of the mountain is the head of Abraham Lincoln. Lincoln was the 16th president. He wrote the Emancipation Proclamation and freed the slaves. He also united our country after the Civil War. In between Lincoln and Jefferson is the head of Theodore Roosevelt. Roosevelt was the 26th president. Roosevelt built the Panama Canal and was known as a great adventurer. He once owned a ranch in Dakota Territory. This territory later split into North Dakota and South Dakota.

This picture shows the three ⇒ presidents next to Washington.

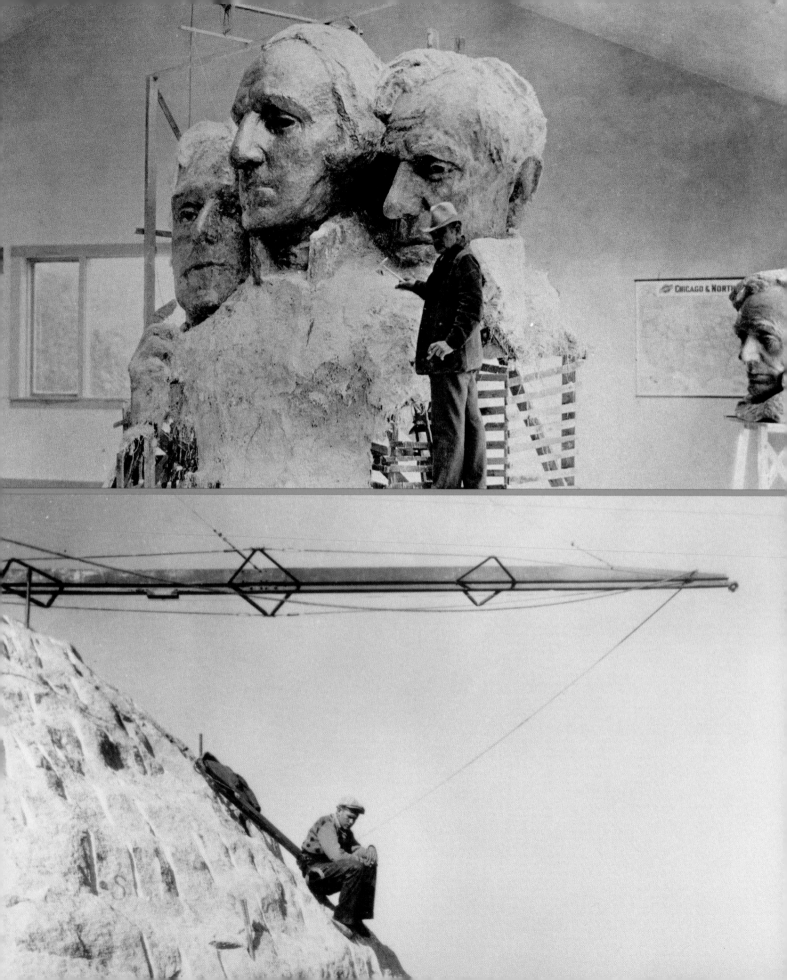

The first step was to make a small **model** of the monument. This model would contain small sculptures of the presidents' heads and faces. Borglum also drew pictures called **sketches** and talked with others about what the monument should look like. He used photographs and paintings to help create the faces. He made small sculptures of each president out of plaster. But how would he make sure the big monument would match the model?

Gutzon invented a measuring tool to measure the model exactly. He measured the noses, ears, eyes, and other features of each face. Gutzon then placed a giant measuring tool on top of Mount Rushmore. He used this tool to mark the exact location of each part of the mountain to be carved. Gutzon and other workers hung from ropes and put marks on the mountain. When Mount Rushmore was all marked, Gutzon and his crew could start the carving!

⇐ **The top photo shows Borglum next to one of the smaller sculptures he used. The bottom picture shows the measuring tool.**

The first step of carving the monument was to remove large chunks of rock from the side of the mountain. Usually people used explosives called **dynamite** to break up rock. Gutzon didn't want to use dynamite because he thought it might destroy the mountain. He tried other ways to break up the rock, but the granite was too hard. He decided he had to use dynamite.

Workers drilled holes into the side of the mountain. Then they put dynamite into the holes and blasted out big chunks of rock. They measured carefully, because they didn't want to make any mistakes. They were able to use Gutzon's measuring tool to know exactly where to drill the holes and put the dynamite.

Once the big chunks of granite were removed, the actual carving of the faces began. At first Gutzon wanted to carve President Jefferson on the southwest side of the mountain. Gutzon studied the mountain and his small model and decided he had to make a change. There wasn't enough rock left on the southwest side of the mountain, so the sculpture of Jefferson had to be moved!

Workers hung from the mountain on ropes and used both hand tools and power tools. They used power drills to drill lots of holes close together. Then they used hammers and chisels to chisel off the rock. Because the granite was so hard, the tools got dull very fast. Every day the tools had to be sharpened. When all the drilling, chiseling, and carving were done, Gutzon inspected the faces. He told the workers to smooth over any rough spots. They used air-powered hammers to do this. When the smoothing was finished, the polished granite looked white.

⇐ **Here you can see workers as they carve Lincoln's face.**

It took only seven years to carve the faces, but it took 14 years for the monument to be completely finished. Gutzon spent most of his time planning and raising money to pay for it. It cost $1 million, which was hard to raise because the country was going through the **Great Depression.** It was a very difficult time for our country, and there wasn't much extra money to give to a project like this. Gutzon went to the U.S. Congress and convinced the government to pay for most of the project.

After the faces were finished, the last step was to finish carving the other areas of the monument. This took two more years. Gutzon himself didn't even see the final monument because he died in March of 1941. His son Lincoln Borglum took over and finished the monument for his father. It was finished on October 31, 1941, less than eight months after Gutzon's death.

⇐ **This picture shows the monument just before it was completed.**

The faces on Mount Rushmore can be seen from 60 miles away. The heads are 60 feet tall. President Washington's nose is 20 feet long, and his eyes are more than 10 feet apart. President Roosevelt's moustache is 21 feet long, which is almost as long as a school bus! A coat and shirt are carved underneath Washington's head. Other details such as ears, nostrils, hair, and eyebrows were carved. Gutzon took special care in carving the eyes because he wanted them to look real.

From up close, you can see lots ⇒ of details in Lincoln's face.

Mount Rushmore has a **studio** or small museum that has Gutzon's sculptures, drawings, and tools used to carve the monument. There is a park called the *Avenue of Flags* at the base of the monument. The park has the flags of all 50 states plus the U.S. territories. Visitors can walk along the Avenue of Flags and then go to trails that head up the mountain.

The area around Mount Rushmore is a national park. It is a beautiful area with streams, trees, and wild animals. About 3 million people visit every year. If you plan a trip to the Black Hills, don't forget to get your picture taken in front of Mount Rushmore!

⇐ **Visitors walk along the Avenue of Flags toward Mount Rushmore.**

Glossary

cathedral (kuh–THEE–drull)
A cathedral is a large church. Gutzon Borglum carved sculptures in a cathedral.

dynamite (DY–nuh–myte)
Dynamite is an explosive that can be used to break things apart. Gutzon Borglum used dynamite to carve Mount Rushmore.

granite (GRA–nit)
Granite is a type of very hard rock. Mount Rushmore is made of light-colored granite.

Great Depression (GRAYT dee–PREH–shun)
The Great Depression was a period of time in the 1930s when many Americans couldn't find jobs. Mount Rushmore was built during the Great Depression.

model (MAH–del)
A model is a small copy of something. Models are sometimes used to plan sculptures.

monument (MAHN–yoo-ment)
A monument is something made in memory of an important person or event. Mount Rushmore is a monument.

peak (PEEK)
A peak is the top of a mountain. Mount Rushmore's peak is 6,000 feet high.

sculptor (SKULP–ter)
An artist who carves statues is a sculptor. A sculptor carved Mount Rushmore.

sketches (SKEH–chez)
Sketches are simple drawings. Sketches were used to plan the faces on Mount Rushmore.

studio (STOO-dee-oh)
A place where artists do their work is a studio. Gutzon Borglum's studio is at Mount Rushmore.

Index

Web Sites

Learn more about Mount Rushmore:

http://www.travelsd.com/rushmore/index.htm

http://www.nps.gov/moru/